Secrets to Writing a Good Essay
30 Days to Essay Writing Success
Step by Step Instructions Included

by

Julie Jones

To learn about the other books I have written which lead to better grades and study skills, click here http://www.beststudentsuccessseries.com.

ISBN:
ISBN-13: 978-0-9842493-4-3
ISBN-10: 0-9842493-4-6
eISBN-13: 978-0-9842493-5-0
eISBN-10: 0-9842493-5-4

Library of Congress Control Number: 2016901326

© www.beststudentsuccessseries.com

DEDICATION

I love you, Victor, my son. You will never know how much I love you and appreciate your help.

PAGE LEFT BLANK INTENTIONALLY

Table of Contents

PAGE LEFT BLANK INTENTIONALLY

Start Here

Thank you

Before we begin, I want to thank you for buying this book. I wrote this book because I found it very difficult to find a way to improve my writing and my son's writing so I wrote this to prevent you from having to research for years how to improve your writing or your child's writing. I have done all the work for you. This is written in a clear concise manner so you can learn to write a 5 paragraph explanatory essay and move on with your life. If you find this book helpful, then tell your friends and family to **buy** my book, and leave positive feedback on Amazon.com. Also, visit my website which is www.beststudentsuccessseries.com to find other books I have written as well as other resources

Who is this book for?

This book is for 10-to-22-year-olds or anyone who wants to know how to write a 5 paragraph explanatory or informative essay especially for the common core or *any* standardized test. It will also make classroom assignments and any homework writing assignments much easier.

How is this book designed?

This book is designed to help you understand how to identify when the writing prompt or assignment requires an explanatory essay, then explains how to write the explanatory essay from start to finish. The chapters are as follows:

1. Review – the Essentials of Writing
2. How to understand a writing prompt
3. Why you should pre-write your essay
4. How to write your outline
5. How to write your essay

After reading this book, you will know how to write a focused, clear and concise 5 paragraph explanatory or informative essay.

Let's Get Started

This book is 36 pages long. You and your child should read the entire book together first. Try to do this in 3 days or less. Just to make sure you both understand everything first. Then, have your child go back to read everything and complete all instructions. Do this in 30 days or less to get the most benefits from the book. To make sure you and your child get everything done in 30 days or less, make sure you mark your calendar for each day you are going to complete an assignment.

Review – the Essentials of Writing

In order for you to get a clear understanding of how to write a 5 paragraph explanatory essay, we must review the following first:

- Basic structure of a sentence
- Listing information or data in a series
- Using transition words
- Basic structure of a paragraph

Understanding how to write at the most basic level will help you as your writing advances because you understand it at its most basic level.

Remember this book gives you the opportunity to get comfortable through practice with writing a 5 paragraph explanatory essay so pay close attention the examples because you will be expected to write or type your own examples as practice or write or type the examples provided as practice. Also, when you get to the review section make sure you write down your answer whether it is in a separate notebook or in this book.

Basic structure of a sentence

According to www.oxforddictionaries.com, a sentence is a set of words that is complete in itself, typically containing a subject and predicate, conveying a statement, question, exclamation, or command, and consisting of a main clause and sometimes one or more subordinate clauses.

A simpler way to look at is a sentence has a subject which is a noun and a predicate which completes the sentence. If you generally speak English without slang, chances are you are probably speaking in complete sentences.

For example, look at the following sentence:

I can ride a bike.

I is the subject or the noun. Can and ride are verbs. Bike is a noun. Another way to look at is, the words **can ride a bike** is a predicate. This is not an in depth explanation of sentence structure, but I just want you to know the basic structure of a sentence.

Listing information or data in a series

When you have to explain two or more things in writing, it is helpful to write the list in a series.

For instance, if I am writing a list of the following fruits:
- Apple
- Pear
- Grape
If I need to explain in a paragraph, I will list it in a series as follows:

apple, pear and grapes

Notice the comma separating each fruit or item. Then, you need to put the word 'and' before the last word or item.

Now that you see how a series looks, let's look at it as it relates to listing details you are going to write about in a paragraph. We are going to discuss an explanatory essay on how to ride a bike in the following chapters so consider the following list:

- Balance yourself on the bike
- Balance yourself and pedal while on the bike
- Learn how to stop the bike

If I need to explain in a paragraph, I will list it in a series in my introductory paragraph as follows:

balance yourself on the bike, balance yourself and pedal while on the bike, and learn how to stop the bike

Do you understand how to make a list in a series? Circle one. **Yes** or **No**. You will need to know this information in order to list what you are going to write about in a paragraph in a series.

Using transition words

What is a transition word? When you move from paragraph to paragraph a transition word helps with the flow from paragraph to paragraph by making it sound like the paragraphs are connected. (See the **Appendix A**. for a list of transition words) A transition word will start each of your 3 body paragraphs.

There are many examples of transition words, but here are the most basic ones that you can't go wrong with using:

1. first, second, third
2. first, next, last

We are going to use these words when you write our 5 paragraph explanatory essay.

Basic structure of a paragraph

There 5 parts to the basic structure of a paragraph. They are the main topic sentence, 3 supporting detail sentences and a summary sentence.

What is a main topic sentence? It tells what the paragraph is about.

What is a supporting detail? It gives details to support the main topic sentence.

What is a summary sentence? A summary sentence gives a summary of what the paragraph was about.

There 3 steps to riding a bicycle. **First**, you must learn how to balance yourself on the bike. **Second**, you must learn how to pedal while balancing yourself on the bike. **Third**, you must learn how to stop on the bike. Riding a bike seems easy, but it is hard to learn. However, once you learn you never forget how to ride a bike.

There 3 steps to riding a bicycle.   **Here is the main topic sentence**.

Here are the 3 supporting detail sentences:

First, you must learn how to balance yourself on the bike. **Second**, you must learn how to pedal while balancing yourself on the bike. **Third**, you must learn how to stop on the bike.

Here are the summary sentences:

Riding a bike seems easy, but it is hard to learn. However, once you learn you never forget how to ride a bike.

In conclusion, this review of the essentials of writing is designed to help you understand writing at its most basic level so that you can improve your writing. Did this review help you? Do you see anything that can help you improve your writing? You will need a clear understanding of these concepts if you expect to learn how to write a 5 paragraph explanatory essay.

Summary:

Please answer the following questions:
Do you know understand the basic structure of a sentence?
Do you understand how to write a list of 3 or more items in a series?
Do you know what transition words are?
Do you know a few words that you can use as transitions?
Do you understand the structure of a paragraph?

If you answered, _no_ to any one of the above questions, then re-read the entire chapter until you can answer yes to each of the above questions. Why? Because it will help build your knowledge so that when you are faced with the situation of writing an explanatory essay, you will know what to do.

If you answered, **yes** to all of the above questions, then we can proceed because you have an action plan in mind of how to write a 5 paragraph explanatory essay. At the end of the chapter, I will review your knowledge. You can use the information in this chapter to answer the questions so it is open-book, but **you** **must** **write the answers down**.

Takeaways:

1) This is an example of writing information in a series:
   - balance yourself on the bike, balance yourself and pedal while on the bike, and learn how to stop the bike
2) This is an example of writing items in a series:
   - apple, pear and grapes
3) By using the following words to transition from by body paragraph to body paragraph, it will help the flow of your essay or paragraph:
   - First
   - Second
   - Third
4) A paragraph must have the following 5 types of sentences to be complete:
   - a main topic sentence or paragraph
   - 3 supporting detail sentences
   - concluding/ summary sentence

Review:

Please answer the following questions _in writing or by typing_:

- What 3 words can you use to transition from each of your 3 body paragraphs?
- How do you list 3 or more items in a series?
- Give an example of a basic sentence?
- What 3 things a basic paragraph must have?

PAGE LEFT BLANK INTENTIONALLY

How do I understand a writing prompt?

In this chapter, I am going to show you how to understand a writing prompt. Understanding a writing prompt is important because it determines how you focus your writing. I am going to show you a writing prompt, define an explanatory or informative essay, tell you what key words to look for and how to determine what information you need to put in your essay.

Here is the writing prompt we are going to discuss:

Writing Situation

Think about when you learned how to ride a bicycle.

Writing Task

Write a 5 paragraph essay to explain how you learned how to write a bicycle.

What is an explanatory or informative essay? An explanatory or informative essay is meant to inform the reader how to do something real or imagined. If it is imagined, your writing must make sense like it is possible.

Think of an explanatory or informative essay as step-by-step instructions such as a box of something you have to put together such as a cell phone, table, bicycle, etc., but in a 5 paragraph form instead of a list.

Figure 1. Example of a list.

Steps to learn how to ride a bicycle
1. Learn how to balance yourself
2. Learn how to pedal the bicycle while balancing yourself
3. Learn how to stop the bicycle

What do I do if I have to write about a topic that I am not interested in or don't know about? In this instance you must use your imagination to write the essay, but make it sound realistic or like something your supporting details could possibly happen. How? By drawing reference from things you have heard on the news, friend's stories, movies you have watched, these are just some examples.

How do I identify whether or not a writing prompt is explanatory or informative? Sometimes the directions will explicitly state that you need to write an explanatory or informative essay. When it is not stated you will need to look for key words such as explain, discuss, tell and how to something.

For example, in the writing prompt it says **explain** and **how** (see below) so in this case you need to explain how to ride a bicycle.

Writing Situation

Think about when you learned how to ride a bicycle.

Writing Task - Explained

Write a 5 paragraph essay to **explain how** you learned how to write a bicycle. **How do I know what I need to focus my writing on?** Some writing prompts have questions in them. In this case you would answer the question by turning the question or questions into a statement. In other instances, where what you need to focus your writing on is not so clear, then look for keywords in the writing prompt which **tells you to explain, discuss, tell, etc.**

For example, this writing prompt is about when I learned how to ride a bicycle so I need to explain step-by-step how I learned how to ride a bicycle, but as a 5 paragraph essay instead on a list which was how step-by-step are usually. To write it as a question, I would say:

How I learned to ride a bicycle step-by-step?

In conclusion, when reading a writing prompt it is important to understand what type of essay you need to write and what questions you need to answer in your writing. These are the keys to focused, clear and concise writing which leads to good grades.

Summary:

Please answer the following questions:
Do you know the purpose of writing an explanatory essay?
Do you know how to turn an explanatory essay writing prompt into a question?
Do you know what words you can look for to identify that the writing prompt is an explanatory essay?
Do you know what information you can use as references to write an explanatory essay if you are not familiar with the subject matter or don't like it?

If you answered, *no* to any one of the above questions, then re-read the entire chapter until you can answer yes to each of the above questions. Why? Because it will help build your knowledge so that when you are faced with the situation of writing an explanatory essay, you will know what to do.

If you answered, *yes* to all of the above questions, then we can proceed because you should have an action plan in mind on how to understand a writing prompt or assignment. At the end of the chapter, I will review your knowledge. You can use the information in this chapter to answer the questions so it is open-book, but *you* <u>must</u> **write the answers down**.

Takeaways:

1) An explanatory or informative essay is meant to inform the reader how to do something real or imagined. If it is imagined, your writing must make sense like it is possible.
2) To identify whether a writing prompt is an explanatory or informative essay when it is not stated explicitly, you need to look for the keywords such as tell, explain, discuss, etc.
3) By turning an explanatory essay into a question before you start writing, you will make your writing more focused and clear.

Review:

Please answer the following questions *in writing or by typing*:

- What can you turn your writing prompt into to make it easier to answer?
- What is the purpose of an explanatory essay?
- What key words can you look for in the writing prompt to identify that it is for an explanatory essay?
- What can you use as references to help improve your writing if you are writing about a subject you are not familiar with or don't know about?

Why is it important that I pre-write or brainstorm in preparation of writing my 5 paragraph explanatory essay?

In the previous chapter, I showed you how to understand and identify an explanatory or informative essay writing prompt. Next, we are going to take about pre-writing or brainstorming for the same writing prompt.

Here is the writing prompt we are going to discuss:

Writing Situation

Think about when you learned how to ride a bicycle.

Writing Task

Write a 5 paragraph essay to explain how you learned how to write a bicycle.

What is pre-writing or brainstorming?   Pre-writing or brainstorming is the process of writing down what first comes to your mind when you are reading the writing prompt without worrying about sequencing. Why is *writing down* what first comes to your mind **important**? There are two reasons:

1) It is easier to organize your thoughts when they are WRITTEN or typed which is very helpful when you are at the outline stage.
2) It is a good way to clear your mind and focus your writing

When pre-writing or brainstorming, you don't write complete sentences. You write just enough so that it triggers your memory about what you want to include in your essay because you want to write as much information down as you can so that you can move on to the next steps of refining your writing. Some of your pre-writing or brainstorming will be relevant and some of it will not be.

Writing Situation

Think about when you learned how to ride a bicycle.

Writing Task

Write a 5 paragraph essay to **explain how** you learned how to write a bicycle.

Pre-writing (Hint: Write the question or questions down that you need to answer in your essay.)

> **Question to answer with pre-writing or brainstorming:** How did I learn how to ride a bicycle step-by-step?
>
> My mom to me took the store to buy a bike
> Asked my uncle to help me learn how to ride my bike
> Get on bike and pedal

In my pre-writing or brainstorming, I only came up with 3 things. The first 2 may or may not be relevant to my essay depending on how I write it, but it definitely doesn't tell you how I learned to ride a bicycle step-by-step. However, the 3rd statement can help.

Get on bike and pedal

Since I already know that it is **not** so easy to get on a bicycle and pedal based on (past experience), I think I can break it down step-by-step to explain how I learned to ride a bicycle. This statement really triggered my memory, as a result, here are some additional statements I am going to add:

> Balance myself on the bicycle
> Balance myself on the bicycle and pedal
> Learn how to stop the bicycle

My **final** pre-writing or brainstorming is as follows:

> How did I learn how to ride a bicycle step-by-step?

> My mom to me took the store to buy a bike
> Asked my uncle to help me learn how to ride my bike
> Get on bike and pedal
> > Balance myself on the bicycle
> > Balance myself on the bicycle and pedal
> > Learn how to stop the bicycle

In conclusion, pre-writing or brainstorming is important to the writing process because it allows you get your thoughts on paper where it is easier to analyze and organize.

Summary:

Please answer the following questions:
Do you know what pre-writing or brainstorming means?
Do you know why it is important to pre-write or brainstorm?

If you answered _no_ to any one of the above questions, then re-read the entire chapter until you can answer yes to each of the above questions. Why? Because it will help build your knowledge so that when you are faced with the situation of writing an explanatory essay, you will know what to do.

If you answered, _yes_ to all of the above questions, then we can proceed because you have an action plan in mind of how to pre-write or brainstorm an essay writing assignment. I will review your knowledge at the end of the chapter. You can use the information in this chapter to answer the questions so it is open-book, but **_you_ must write the answers down**.

Takeaways:

1) Pre-writing or brainstorming is the process of writing down what first comes to your mind when you are reading the writing prompt without worrying about sequencing.
2) To identify whether a writing prompt is an explanatory or informative essay when it is not stated explicitly, you need to look for the keywords such as tell, explain, discuss, etc.
3) Pre-writing or brainstorming is important because it helps you organize your thoughts and clears your mind so that you can focus your writing

Review:

Please answer the following questions in writing or by typing:

- What is pre-writing or brainstorming?
- Why is pre-writing or brainstorming important?

How do I write an outline for my 5 paragraph explanatory essay?

In the previous lesson, we learn how pre-writing or brainstorming can help you focus your writing. We are going to learn how to write an outline for your explanatory or informative essay. By creating an outline that is reflective of a 5 paragraph essay with an introduction, 3 supporting detail and conclusion.

Outline

What is an outline? An outline gives a brief explanation of what you are going to write about in an essay or paragraph in list form. It doesn't have to be in complete sentences unless you have instruction otherwise.

Why is it important to write and outline? An outline helps you organize your thoughts in list form and helps you see what you are going to write about. If this doesn't make sense don't worry, you will understand better as you read more and review the examples that I have provided.

Introduction

What is an introduction? The purpose of writing an introduction to an essay is to inform the reader what he/ she will learn while reading the essay while including the answers to the writing prompt. As a result, your writing will be focused and clear to the reader.

Remember: Think of an introduction to an essay as the paragraph which informs the reader what he/ she will learn in **your** essay as it relates to the topic of the writing prompt

Introduction: Contains the question I must answer in my essay and the answers I will expand on in your essay. Think what the reader will learn in **your** essay.

Question: How to learn how to ride a bicycle step-by-step?
Answers: Learn how to balance yourself on the bicycle. Learn how to balance yourself and pedal, learn how to stop the bicycle without crashing

Answers: Must be able to expand on your answers as supporting details. You need at least 3 high level answers so that you can provide supporting details

Body Paragraph

What is a body paragraph? A body paragraph has its own main topic sentence and at 3 supporting detail sentences and supports or refers back to the main topic or introduction as it relates to the writing prompt or assignment.

Supporting Detail

What is a supporting detail? Supporting details of a paragraph **explain** the what, where, when, why and how of the main topic or question answered regarding the writing prompt.

How do the supporting details explain or the support the main topic or questions answered in the essay?   The following types of information can be used to provide supporting details:

- Explain how something happened and where
- Define words
- Give examples
- State the location, times and dates of events

1. *Body paragraph #1 main topic sentence*: Learn how to balance yourself on the bicycle
   - *Supporting details #1 for body paragraph #1*
     a) Takes practice
     b) Not simple as sitting on the bicycle while feet on the ground
2. *Body paragraph #2 main topic sentence:* Learn how to balance yourself and pedal
   - *Supporting details #2 for body paragraph #2*
     a) Must do two things at once
     b) Takes practice
3. *Body paragraph #2 main topic sentence:* Learn how to stop the bicycle without crashing
   - *Supporting details #3 for body paragraph #3*
     a) Must do two things at once
     b) Breaks versus no breaks

After reviewing the information, I wrote for my body paragraph and supporting details as an outline, I see that will not have enough information or details to write at 3 – 5 sentences as supporting details.   I am glad I wrote the outline in an essay format because it helps to focus my writing and helps me to see if I need to develop my details further before I write my essay. Don't worry about the amount of time it takes because the more experience you get with writing the better you will be and the quicker you will get with organizing your thoughts.

Three things:
   1. Good, I **wrote** down the outline
   2. Good, I wrote down the outline in an essay format
   3. Good, I noticed that I need to add more details to my outline before I start writing the essay.

Here is my revised supporting detail section for my outline:

1. Equipment needed
   a) Knee pads
   b) Helmet
   c) Bicycle
2. Pick a Location
   a) Park or empty parking lot
   b) concrete
3. Learn how to balance yourself on the bicycle
   a) Takes practice
   b) Not simple as sitting on the bicycle while feet on the ground
4. Learn how to balance yourself and pedal
   a) Must do two things at once
   b) Takes practice
5. Learn how to stop the bicycle without crashing
   a) Must do two things at once
   b) Breaks versus no breaks

Conclusion

What is a conclusion? A conclusion does 2 things:

a) Restates the introduction of the essay in different words
b) Informs the reader what he/ she should have learned in the essay

How does the conclusion restate the introduction of the paragraph and inform the reader what he/ she should have learned in the essay? A conclusion can tell the reader what he/ she should have learned in the essay by doing the following:

- Summarizing what the entire essay was about (Hint: use synonyms for the answers to the writing prompt)
- Stating what the reader should know about the main topic as a result of reading the essay

> Conclusion: riding a bicycle is hard, you think about safety and it can be a long process.

This is my final outline. It contains all of the information I need to right a focused 5 paragraph **essay.**

Question: How to learn how to ride a bicycle step-by-step?
Answers: Learn how to balance yourself on the bicycle, learn how to balance yourself and pedal, learn how to stop the bicycle without crashing

1) Equipment needed

        a) Knee pads
        b) Helmet
        c) Bicycle
  2) Pick a Location
        a) Park or empty parking lot
        b) concrete
  3) Learn how to balance yourself on the bicycle
        a) Takes practice
        b) Not simple as sitting on the bicycle while feet on the ground
  4) Learn how to balance yourself and pedal
        a) Must do two things at once
        b) Takes practice
  5) Learn how to stop the bicycle without crashing
        a) Must do two things at once
        b) Breaks versus no breaks

Conclusion: riding a bicycle is hard, you think about safety and it can be a long process.

By creating an outline before I start writing my 5 paragraph essay, I can save time, focus my writing and organize my thoughts.

Summary:

Please answer the following questions:
Do you know what an outline is?
Do you know why it is important to write an outline?
Do you know what an introduction is?
Do you know what supporting details are?
Do you know what is a conclusion?

If you answered **no** to any one of the above questions, then re-read entire chapter until you can answer yes to each of the above questions. Why? Because it will help build your knowledge so that when you are faced with the situation of writing an explanatory essay, you will know what to do.

If you answered, **yes** to all of the above questions, then we can proceed because you have an action plan in mind of how to write an outline for a 5 paragraph explanatory essay. At the end of the chapter, I will review your knowledge. You can use the information in this chapter to answer the questions so it is open-book, but **you** **must** **write the answers down**.

Takeaways:
1) An outline is what you are going to write about in an essay or paragraph in list form

2) An outline helps you organize your thoughts list form and helps you see what you are going to write about
3) Supporting details of a paragraph explain the what, where, when, why and how of the main topic or question answered regarding the writing prompt.
4) To provide supporting details, you can do the following:
   - Explain how something happened and where
   - Define words
   - Give examples
   - State the location, times and dates of events
5) A conclusion restates the introduction of the essay in different words and informs the reader what he/ she should have learned in the essay

Review:

Please answer the following questions *in writing or by typing*:

- What is an outline?
- Why it is important to write an outline?
- What is an introduction?
- What are supporting details?
- What is a conclusion?

How do I write my 5 paragraph explanatory essay?

In the previous chapter, we learned that an outline can help us organize our thoughts. We are finally going to write the explanatory essay using the introduction, 3 body paragraphs with supporting details and conclusion that we created in the outline.

Question: How to learn how to ride a bicycle step-by-step?
Answers: equipment needed, pick a location, learn how to balance yourself on the bicycle, learn how to balance yourself and pedal, learn how to stop the bicycle without crashing

    1) Equipment needed
       a) Knee pads
       b) Helmet
       c) Bicycle
    2) Pick a Location
       a) Park or empty parking lot
       b) concrete
    3) Learn how to balance yourself on the bicycle
       a) Takes practice
       b) Not simple as sitting on the bicycle while feet on the ground
    4) Learn how to balance yourself and pedal
       a) Must do two things at once
       b) Takes practice
    5) Learn how to stop the bicycle without crashing
       a) Must do two things at once
       b) Breaks versus no breaks

Conclusion: riding a bicycle is hard, you think about safety and it can be a long process.

Introduction

From Outline

Question: How to learn how to ride a bicycle step-by-step?
Answers: equipment needed, pick a location, learn how to balance yourself on the bicycle. Learn how to balance yourself and pedal, learn how to stop the bicycle without crashing

Outline in paragraph form

Do you think learning to how to ride is easy? This couldn't be further from the truth. You can simply get on a bicycle and ride. You have to think about safety, how to balance yourself on your bicycle, how to balance yourself on your bicycle while pedaling and how to stop without crashing your bicycle.

Supporting detail #1

From Outline

1. Safety
    a) Equipment needed
    b) Pick a location

Outline in paragraph form

First, you need to think about safety. Depending on where you live, there are laws which require that you wear a helmet and knee pads when riding a bicycle including while you are learning. Even if it is not the law in your state, it is a good idea to wear a helmet and knee pads for safety reasons. A lot of falling down takes place before you actually learn to ride a bicycle and this equipment can help prevent some bruises.

Body paragraph # 2 and Supporting details for it

From Outline
1) Learn how to balance yourself on the bicycle
   a) Takes practice
   b) Not simple as sitting on the bicycle while feet on the ground

Outline in paragraph form

Next, you have to learn how to balance yourself on the bicycle and pedal. You can start by sitting on the bicycle with both feet on the ground. Then, you can start trying to pedal one foot at a time until you are able to pedal without falling.

Supporting detail #3

From Outline
4) Learn how to balance yourself and pedal
   c) Must do two things at once

            d) Takes practice
        5) Learn how to stop the bicycle without crashing
            c) Must do two things at once
            d) Breaks versus no breaks

Outline in paragraph form

Third, you have to learn how to stop your bicycle without crashing. If
your bicycle has breaks, then you are lucky because it will be easier to
learn how to stop the bicycle without brakes. However, if you don't have
breaks, then you will have to learn how stop your bicycle with your feet
while balancing yourself.

Conclusion

From Outline

   Riding a bicycle is hard, you have think safety and it can be a long
   process

Outline in paragraph form

In conclusion, learning how to ride a bike isn't easy. You will have to
learn how to do several things at once such as balancing, pedaling and
stopping on the bicycle.

Here is my final draft of my essay:

Do you think learning to how to ride is easy? This couldn't be further
from the truth. You can simply get on a bicycle and ride. You have to
think about safety, how to balance yourself on your bicycle, how to
balance yourself on your bicycle while pedaling and how to stop without
crashing your bicycle.

First, you need to think about safety. Depending on where you live,
there are laws which require that you wear a helmet and knee pads
when riding a bicycle including while you are learning. Even if it is not
the law in your state, it is a good idea to wear a helmet and knee pads
for safety reasons. A lot of falling down takes place before you actually

learn to ride a bicycle and this equipment can help prevent some bruises.

Next, you have to learn how to balance yourself on the bicycle and pedal. You can start by sitting on the bicycle with both feet on the ground. Then, you can start trying to pedal one foot at a time until you are able to pedal without falling.

Third, you have to learn how to stop your bicycle without crashing. If your bicycle has breaks, then you are lucky because it will be easier to learn how to stop the bicycle without brakes. However, if you don't have breaks, then you will have to learn how stop your bicycle with your feet while balancing yourself.

In conclusion, learning how to ride a bike isn't easy. You will have to learn how to do several things at once such as balancing, pedaling and stopping on the bicycle.

Summary:

Please answer the following questions:
Do you understand how to write a clear, concise 5 paragraph explanatory essay now?
Do you understand how to put it together from understanding the writing prompt so that you answer the right questions?
Do you understand how to write and/ or rewrite a quick outline to map out or layout your thoughts in a clear, concise manner?
Do you understand how to write your outline in paragraph form for the introduction, 3 body paragraphs, and conclusion?

If you answered, *no* to any one of the above questions, then re-read all the worksheets starting with understanding the writing prompt until you can answer yes to each of the above questions. Why? Because it will help build your knowledge so that when you are faced with the situation of writing an explanatory essay, you will know what to do.

If you answered, *yes* to all of the above questions, then we can proceed because you have an action plan in mind of how to write a 5 paragraph explanatory essay. At the end of the chapter, I will review your knowledge. You can use the information in this chapter to answer the questions so it is open-book, but ***you* <u>must</u> write the answers down**.

Takeaways:

1) Use keywords to identify what type of essay you need to write
2) Turn your writing prompt into a question to focus your writing
3) Pre-writing or brainstorming will help organize your thoughts and clear your mind to focus your writing
4) Writing an outline can help you organize your thoughts
5) Use your outline to write your essay in paragraph form

Review:

Please answer the following questions _in writing or by typing_:
- How do you understand a writing prompt?
- What is pre-writing?
- What is the purpose of an outline?

Lessons Learned

Now that you have learned the system to write a 5 paragraph explanatory essay, I hope that you found this book easy to understand. Do you understand that writing is a process and your final essay may look different at different stages? Do you feel that you learned how to write a 5 paragraph explanatory essay? I hope your answer is yes. Do you think you will use the book as a reference? I hope your answer is yes.

Next, please go to my website which is beststudentsuccessseries.com. It offers more writing courses and points you to references which will help you improve your writing.

In order to improve your writing, I recommend that you look at this book as a good starting point and read my other books.

I shared with you my system on writing a 5 paragraph explanatory essay. It helped me to learn how to improve my writing and as a result I started speaking more clearly. I hope that you notice the same in yourself. Please your comments about your results on amazon.com and on my website.

Appendix A - Transition Words

Transition words help control the flow as a person writes or reads from paragraph to paragraph to make it clear as well as smooth. Here are a few transitions you can use.

in the first place
not only ... but also
as a matter of fact
in like manner
in addition
coupled with
in the same fashion / way
first, second, third
in the light of
not to mention
to say nothing of
equally important
by the same token
again
to
and
also
then
equally
identically
uniquely
like
as
too
moreover
as well as
together with
of course
likewise
comparatively
correspondingly
similarly
furthermore
additionally

www.ingramcontent.com/pod-product-compliance
Lightning Source LLC
Chambersburg PA
CBHW060803270326
41926CB00002B/73